# Knock Knock,
# Who's God?

# Knock Knock, Who's God?

Nigel Linacre

BOOKS

Winchester, UK
Washington, USA

First published by O-Books, 2011
O-Books is an imprint of John Hunt Publishing Ltd., Laurel House, Station Approach,
Alresford, Hants, SO24 9JH, UK
office1@o-books.net
www.o-books.com

For distributor details and how to order please visit the 'Ordering' section on our website.

Text copyright: Nigel Linacre 2009

ISBN: 978 1 84694 815 2

A CIP catalogue record for this book is available from the British Library.

Design: Stuart Davies

Printed in the UK by CPI Antony Rowe
Printed in the USA by Offset Paperback Mfrs, Inc

We operate a distinctive and ethical publishing philosophy in all
areas of our business, from our global network of authors to
production and worldwide distribution.

*To my Father*

# Hello God

*May I say hello?*

Anytime

*Thank you for being here*

I couldn't not be

*Thank you for listening*

Always do

*And for letting me be me*

How would you like to be?

~

# Opportunity

*OK, God, who are you?*

You call me God

*And what is that?*

What do you say it is?

*We are going round in circles*

We are establishing some basics

*Give me something new*

I am the uncaused cause

~

# The Cause

*And me, who am I?*

You are part of the caused.

*OK, you are the cause and we are*
*the caused*

Except that I am also the caused

*I thought that is us*

What is of me cannot not be me

*Except that it can feel that way*

It can feel so many ways

~

# The One and the Many

*So you are the one and we are the many*

But the one and the many are all one

*Even when the many do not know*

They know what they know

*Life is constantly changing*

That is life

*From not knowing to knowing*

To knowing what you know

~

# Who are you?

*How do I know you are God?*
How do you know anything?
*You could just be a fragment of my
personality*
I am a fragment of your personality
*You know what I mean*
You are reaching out and I am here
*So there is no need to reach that far*
I am here now, always

~

# Deal

*I know it's you because you are always*
*here?*
I am
*Unless you are not*
I am. Always
*And so am I. We have something*
*in common.*
We have a great deal in common.
*Like what?*
Like this. Isn't existence a great deal?

~

# The Gift

*I would say existence is a gift*
And what are you going to do with
that gift?
*By and large I have tended to do what*
*pleases me*
And what is wrong with that?
*I would like to do that which*
*pleases you*
Why is that preferable to you?
*You can take rather more into account*
And how are you going to do that?

~

# Time and Space

*I have to create some time and space*

You have plenty of time and space!

*I have to create some inner space*

*and listen*

The "space" is always here

*I have to allow myself to be changed*

How is that?

*I have to let go of who I am not*

And become who you already are

~

# Walking

*And I have to ask?*

For what do you have to ask?

*I have to ask for guidance*

As to what you should ask for?

*Yes, that's where to start.*

What would you ask for if you

knew what to ask for?

*I would ask to walk with you more of*

*the time*

You are always walking with me.

~

# Presence

*I mean walk with more awareness of you*
You don't know I am here?
*I mean feel your presence. That state*
*of grace.*
And what will you do for that?
*I will ask for it.*
And?
*You will give it.*
So what else is there to discuss?

~

# Imperfection

*I would like it to be equally easy for*

*everyone*

It is

*It hasn't usually seemed that way to me*

You have cut yourself off

*I know, it is my fault*

It's been your choice

*OK, temporarily*

Everything is temporary

~

# Guidance

*I would ask for more*

Then why don't you?

*I ask for your continual guidance*

And what is your part in this?

*I will listen*

Is that all?

*Oh, and following through!*

You are serious?

~

# Hearing

*But how will I know it is you?*

You can tell

*Tell what?*

Tell what is uplifting

*It's true. Your stuff has a*
*certain tonality*

You are listening

*But it is not always easy to hear*

Cut out the background noise

~

# Working

*I am not sure the world is working*
*so well*
And how would you like it to work?
*With more love and flow*
And what are you going to do
about it?
*Bring more love and flow*
So what is not working?
*You seem to have left us in charge*
I haven't entirely gone away

~

# Something

*What if I knew that the whole thing*
*was perfect?*
Sometimes you do
*And sometimes I fret.*
Indeed you do
*But suppose I would know, always.*
*It feels close*
As close as you wish
*Yet something holds me back*
What is that?

~

# The Path

*Not knowing what I should aim for*

The path is clear

*I don't see it*

But you are starting to feel it

*Maybe that is true. Can I see it?*

Yes, you can. It's called your

imagination

*But that is just my imagination*

Actually, it is ours

~

# Past

*You are in my imagination?*

Where would you have me be?

*Yes, there certainly*

OK

*But when you are everywhere, I wonder*

*where I am*

You are where you are

*I mean, what is left for me.*

And what would you like to be left

for you?

~

# Present

*Less and less, something and nothing:*
*a space*
Which is what you have. You are
inhabiting a space
*That doesn't feel like me, I feel much*
*more real than that*
I didn't say you are a space; you are
inhabiting one
*So what is the me in the space?*
Like you said: something
and nothing
*This is getting a little mysterious*
It is not so hard to sense

~

# Drama

*Can we bring this drama to life?*

I already have.

*And what have you done?*

The unchanging has brought the
changing to life

*And I am an aspect of the changing?*

Yes, but you are beginning to sense
the unchanging

*The common thread that runs through
all things*

The divine drama continues

~

# Unchanging

*When I sense the unchanging, the*
*changing doesn't matter*
Oh but it is matter. It is matter
that changes
*Yes, but the reassurance of continuity is*
*ever-present*
Weren't you going to ask
about death?
*Yes, and I know your answer*
There is no death
*You could have fooled me*
And there is death in every moment

~

# Death

*OK, death, yes or no?*
No, not in the sense that you
mean it
*Meaning?*
Consciousness, energy, and
matter continue
*So I am an eternal being*
Everything dies. Every form dies.
You can see this
*Now I am more confused than ever*
There's more to come

~

# Light

*Hit me with it*

You are not really real

*I feel really real to me*

Your essence is. But your form

is temporary

*This body, character, personality?*

Yes, it is temporal

*I thought I was an eternal being of light*

You are

~

# Lifes

*My hopes for eternal life keep going up*
*and down*
What if you could have it your way?
*I would be me for as long as that*
*was purposeful*
And then?
*I might like to go have a very*
*different experience*
As a human being or in
another realm
*Why not one followed by the other?*
Why not, then?

~

# Changes

*But will I still be me?*

Is your character the same as when
you were 10?

*No, I guess not. Has it died?*

Call it what you will. One form
replaces another

*So changing-me is constantly birthing
and dying*

But there is another you?

*The unchanging me*

By comparison with the you that
you know, yes

~

# Selves

*But this deeper me, does it change?*

It has experiences, it knows who it is

*And I don't?*

You are still confusing self with self

*Do you mean the self we observe and*

*the self that observes?*

The observed and the observer

*Objective and subjective*

Handy as that is, I mean more

than that

~

# Observers

*So which self are we on about?*

You are already familiar with

observed and observer

*Yes, I get that*

So now let me introduce the

observer of the observer

*Does this go on forever?*

How does the observer differ from

the observed?

*The observer is much more aware*

So is the observer of the observer

you know

~

# Intent

*So there is a self I don't yet know*
What do you think?
*But how can it be me if I don't even
know it?*
But it is, you do, you will remember
*No doubt?*
It cannot not be this way
*I will reunite with my self*
You will become whole

~

# Ready

*I remain a trifle confused about death*

There's plenty more to come

*After this incarnation, there is plenty*
*more to come?*

Yes, there is plenty more to come

*How can I prepare for that?*

The same way you are preparing
for this

*How's that?*

Getting yourself together

~

# Three selves

*Don't think I am there yet*

You still think you are you

*I thought we had got me: three selves*

*in one*

That's a temporary construction

*So who am I?*

In reality, there is no I

*So I don't even exist?*

You do, but as something

much grander

~

# Figment

*OK, once more with feeling: who am I?*
A figment of my imagination
*Well please continue imagining*
A part of me
*Joined to you*
Let me say that again - you are a
part of me
*What's the difference?*
There is no you and me – just we

~

# Oh, brother

*So I don't really exist but we do exist?*

Everything is connected – the
whole caboodle

*I really am my brother*

What you give, you also get

*Giving is its own reward*

What goes around comes around

*There's just one show*

There are a billion shows

~

# Restart

*I don't know where to restart*

Oh yes you do

*I have to get myself ready*

Take our time

*OK, I am here to serve*

And how would you like to do that?

*Let's talk about religion*

Everyone finds their own path

~

# Religions

*All religions are equally good?*

Any religion may be helpful or
unhelpful

*So how do we choose between them?*

Religions aren't me

*The map is not the territory it tries
to describe*

OK, religions are spiritual maps

*And their accuracy depends on the map
makers' skills*

And their value on the map
reader's reading

~

# Religious Interpretation

*So religion is in the mind of the*
*map-reader*
Religious interpretation is in their
mind
*And there are many interpretations*
As there are many paths
*So all religions can be equally helpful?*
What would a helpful religion
look like?
*It would enable being close to you*
And how would it do that?

~

# Helpful Religions

*It would create attractive space*
And what else would helpful
religions do?
*Act as a spur to spiritual development*
You would know a tree by its fruits
*And social development too*
Don't all religions do this?
*Yes, but they do lots of unhelpful*
*stuff too*
Just like human beings

~

# Religious Exclusivity

*But some religions say theirs is the*
*only path*
It may be the only path that feels
right for them
*But they can't all be right*
Why not? Do they have to
be wrong?
*How could they each be*
*exclusively right?*
There is only one God
*OK*
So who do they think they are
following?

~

# Real thing

*Judge not?*

The truth is plain

*But many religions are going through*
*the motions*

As are many non-religions

*But if they think it's the real thing and*
*it isn't?*

They are the real thing

*You are the real thing*

Everlasting

~

# Jesus

*Can we talk about Jesus?*

Why not talk to Jesus?

*How can that be arranged?*

You think mine is the only voice?

*"I am the way, the truth and the life":*

*is he?*

In essence, yes

*Wow, so the Christians are on a*

*great path*

Not exclusively

~

# The Way

*How does that work?*

Being one with the way, you are

the way

*And how does one become that?*

Being one with the truth, you are

the truth

*And the truth shall set you free!*

Being one with life, you are the life

*One being*

Which does not make anyone else

not one being

~

# The One

But *"No-one comes to the father except*
*via me"*
Jesus is one with all-that-is
*So everything comes via him*
There is no way to all-that-is except
by all-that-is
*So he's the one*
Yes, he's the one
*So that's pretty clear*
And he's not the only one who is
the one

~

# Maps

*What about Buddhism, Hinduism,*
*Islam?*
Maps, glorious maps
*Worth exploring*
Explore as you will
*Will I find you there?*
You will find your construction of
me there
*Is that who I am dealing with here too?*
What do you think?

~

# Construct

*I would like to get past my construct, to*
*the real you*
Then you have to get past your self
*That sounds easier said than done*
You have to cease to be yourself
*That doesn't sound so good*
You have to cease to be your
separate self
*That sounds better*
And be one with me

~

# Following

*Oneness is OK for Jesus, but not for us*
He said, "Follow me"
*As our leader. Jesus shows us how*
It wasn't just a show. He came to
show the way
*That we might worship him*
That you may follow him
*And adore him?*
And come where he has come

~

# Step

*Well that should be easy*
You have been shown the way
*I have been shown an idea*
And I am with you always
*And that is supremely comforting*
This is a joint effort
*I don't feel ready*
One step at a time

~

# Becoming

*Is there anything else I need to know?*

There is nothing you need to know

*So what is the point?*

Being

*Being is the point of being*

Being and becoming

*Which is really more being*

Being is the point

~

# Here now

*Can you be a bit more precise*
*about being?*
Being here now
*As opposed to being somewhere else?*
Being in the future, being in the past
*Imagination and memory*
All imagination. And being
somewhere else
*Like where?*
Stuck inside your head

~

# Connecting

*Is that where I am most of the time?*

Your thinking takes you round
in circles

*What else can we do: feel?*

Be; Be centred; Be calm;
Be connected.

*It sounds like a recipe for taking it easy*

Why take it hard?

*There's so much to do*

There's nothing to do

~

# Lilies

*Please explain nothing to do*
For you, doing implies force. Why
not flow?
*What's the difference?*
In flow there is no force: no doing to
*Just being with?*
Connecting with others, with flow,
with oneness
*That's generally enough*
The lilies of the valley, they do
not toil

~

# Peak experience

*So when I am flowing, I am not
really doing?*
When you're in the flow, it won't
feel like doing
*Like a "peak experience"*
All the time
*That would be great. Would we get
anything done?*
Life is growth. It is always growing
*But we have to act*
Why do you want to do it
your way?

~

# Trust

*I think the issue is trust*
Trusting you or trusting me?
*And the habits of many years*
And connection
*Connecting with what?*
Connecting with me, with life
*This is a habit I can practice*
How's it going so far?
~

# Dive

*Doing stuff on my own feels like a fight*
You want to fight?
*Working with you feels flowful*
So why not do it all the time?
*That feels like a big step up?*
Take it gradually
*You know I like to dive in*
And jump back out

~

# Sense

*So this feels like it is it!*

You are it

*I mean this feels like the path*

You were never off the path

*I felt way off track*

You just weren't moving

*Standing by the side of the road*

Waiting for a pick-up truck

~

# Expand

*But you were there always*
So who was waiting for who?
*I see that, I get that. Now I*
*am travelling*
Now you are surrendering
*The idea of surrendering makes me*
*feel sad*
For you, it means losing
*But is it really gaining?*
It is really losing: losing yourself
~

# Jump

*Wow, and that feels like jumping*
*into nothing*
You will have to jump
*Have to? No choice?*
What do you think happens when
you die?
*You know we don't talk about death*
You are in denial
*But it is going to happen?*
And what do you think happens
then?

~

# Space

*A giant leap for man, a small step*
*for mankind!*
A leap into a space
*A different kind of space. Does*
*death matter?*
There is no death, only change
*OK*
We've been here before
*So we can look forward to the afterlife*
Well that depends

~

# Next life

*On heaven or hell?*

Cause and effect

*Meaning?*

One life leads to another

*One life affects another?*

Would you have it any different?

*Anything else?*

Your state of consciousness

is primary

~

# Where

*And what is that state of*
*consciousness?*
It is how you are being you
*That is what we carry forward?*
You see what happens to the rest
*So that is what I have to work on?*
That is what we have to work on
*And how do we do that?*
Together

~

# We

*So this is about trust?*

This is about being more than you

*Stopping being me?*

Being we

*A dance into the unknown*

A gradual evolution

*Surrendering*

And growing

~

# Complete

*At times like this, everything else*
*seems pointless*
Pointless but whole, complete
*And yet there are so many ways to*
*spur growth*
Completely, Amen, Inshallah,
it grows
*So what do I get to do?*
You still want to go your own way?
*Only when I lose it*
Then it's important to work together

~

# Choice

*OK, every day we work together*
Every minute
*No peace for the wicked*
No disturbance for the devout
*It's another way to be*
So what's your choice
*Every minute, every instance*
With the occasional holiday?

~

# Zig

*You know I enjoy some feelings*
*of separateness*
They provide contrast
*A zig before a zag*
For how long do you want to go
on zig-zagging?
*I am happy with rather more zig*
*these days*
So be it
*And if I lose you?*
I will be here

~

# Sin

*Can we talk about sin?*

Falling short. Why would you fall?

*In order to get back up again*

Then it is not really sin, is it?

*But it can hurt*

And what is pain?

*Something to be avoided*

A summoning of help

~

# Believing

*So what is my life about?*

What would you like it to be about?

*That's it? It's all choice?*

There's a core curriculum

*And what is that about?*

Discovery and growth

*And making a difference?*

Your growth makes a difference

~

# Mountain

*I thought contribution was primary*
It is. You are. You make it
through being
*Being who?*
Being yourself
*That should be easy enough*
Being your greater self
*And who on earth is that?*
Not on earth

~

# Off the earth

*How can I be on earth and not
on earth?*
You are in both places
simultaneously
*It feels like I am here*
A part of you is here, a part of you
is apart
*I have to reunite with that?*
As we have said, you have to
become one
*One with everything*
Become one with yourself

~

# Why

*And how do I do that?*

Go within, listen, breathe, imagine

*What would I imagine?*

Imagine your greater self,

talk together

*Can everyone do this?*

Yes, but not everyone wants to

do this

*Or is even remotely aware*

You said it

~

# Awareness

*So we are back to becoming aware?*

Awareness is who you are

*I thought we were consciousness*

Conscious awareness

*So we become more when we are*

*more aware*

And what you are aware of

*So we are not just conscious beings*

Subject, awareness and object are

one

~

# Need

*This feels completely, convincingly real*
That's how it is meant to be
*That, life, and this experience here now*
It's a convincing illusion
*I am happy to be a part of it*
Would you be happy to be the
whole of it?
*I will settle for a small part*
And that is why you are here now
~

# Planned

*So it is all preplanned*
Not from your perspective
*I experience the illusion of choice*
They are real choices, made within
the illusion
*You have preplanned the whole thing*
It all unfolds
*And you can see the whole thing*
You just said you did not want to

~

# Contribution

*When did I do that?*

When you said you wanted a

small part

*I could have chosen the whole thing?*

Yes, you still can

*That's the end*

The river flows into the sea

*Let me flow gently*

It's your river

~

# Perfect

*I can only take on so much*
Your life has been perfect for you
*I haven't led a perfect life*
No, but your life has been perfect
for you
*I thought it was about winning*
*and losing*
And it isn't?
*No, it is about joining and becoming*
Then so it shall be

~

# Guarantee

*I thought I was learning the lessons*
*of survival*
You have life in abundance
*We manage to make quite a lot of noise*
*about it*
You are not alone
*But in the myth the individual has to*
*battle it out*
And you have done a lot of battling
*I proved I could stand on my own*
And what are you going to
prove next?

~

# Prove

*I don't have to prove anything!*

And why is that?

*Because I am!*

You are what?

*I am being and that's enough*

And

*I am not alone*

It's good to hear you say that

~

# Creating

*So it's us*
And us is?
*You and me and everything*
And would you go to war
with yourself?
*No more winning, no more losing,*
*just living*
Creating
*Enjoying being*
Co-creating

~

# Flowing

*This living thing may not be so difficult*
*after all*
It isn't
*When I am flowing*
When we are flowing together
*Going with the flow*
Feel it. Neat, isn't it
*I'm there*
You're close

~

# Fullness

*What takes me away from you?*
You take yourself away from me
*And how do I do that?*
You look the other way
*And what do I see?*
You do not see life in its fullness
*I see a particular situation*
You see yourself being separate

~

# Separation

*That's the point: separation*
From which all fears spring
*I thought fear was the problem*
It is the effect of separation
*And the cause of virtually*
*every problem*
We shall overcome
*But it has given us something to do*
And look at what you have done

~

# Top

*OK, we haven't exactly done that well*
You are at a fairly basic level
*Hasn't mankind climbed to the top of*
*the tree?*
Which tree would that be?
*The tree of planetary disruption*
You have been behaving recklessly
for sometime
*It's almost as if we don't care*
You don't

~

# Fighting

*OK, I renounce it all*

You renounce what?

*Whatever I am doing to make this mess*

Every thought? Every feeling?

Every action?

*That sounds like a lot. I would like to*

*make a start*

Stop fighting

*OK, can do*

With yourself

~

# Enough

*OK, I get that*
You don't think that way
*No, I am still imagining survival*
And what you imagine turns up
*How do I, how do we get beyond that?*
Recognise you have enough
*OK*
And notice how the world works

~

# Works

*How does it work?*

You get what you radiate

*Fighting begets fighting?*

Love begets love

*Winning begets losing*

Giving creates giving

*We know this*

Start doing it

~

# There

*So that is what we are to do*

That is who you are to be

*And who is that?*

That's your choice

*And what is that?*

The one you are going to make

*And if we make the wrong one?*

I will be there, either way

~

# Imagination

*Even so, we may not know you*

And yet you may

*We may imagine we are on our own*

You may imagine me

*Is that what I am doing now?*

Imagination is a doorway to

understanding

*But is it real?*

It is the creator of reality

~

# Specifics

*I have been asking for guidance*
And
*Feeling I am being guided*
*without specifics*
You don't call this specific?
*It is, but thank you for the feeling too*
You are tuning in a little more
*There's a long way to go?*
As far as you would like to

~

# Lots

*All the way, please, gradually*
And that's where you are
*With the option to stop anytime*
That's where you stop
*And get back on*
You have got it
*So what is difficult about this?*
It isn't

~

# Peace

*Thank you for every moment*
*of attention*
You bring it on yourself
*The sense of rhythm and flow*
Are always here, look
around, breathe
*And in every moment there is peace*
That passeth understanding
*This is experiential rather than*
*intellectual*
This is life in all its glory
~

# Trustless

*I am wondering what else I need*

We've covered this. Nothing

*Food and drink*

You don't think it is coming?

*But even when it is, we worry that*

*it isn't?*

And that's down to?

*We are learning one snack at a time*

You behave as though you lack trust

~

# Breath

By and large, we don't trust
one another
And that is because?
We don't trust ourselves
Or me
Yes, that must be true: we don't
trust you
On what evidence?
Of our lives?
Every breath is guaranteed

~

# Rest

*Until our last*

The guarantee is renewable

*There may be pain along the way*

Life ebbs and flows

*I know, and you are there*

But this changes everything

*And how is that?*

I will give you rest

~

# Worry

*I feel that afresh*
Experience it
*How do I do that?*
Surrender every burden
*Does that mean giving up?*
Give them up to me
*You will take them on?*
You are weary

~

# Hook

*Does that mean I am off the hook?*

You were never on the hook

*I was hooked on action: Action*

*Anonymous!*

There is still room for creation

*Not re-action. But most "creation"*

*is reaction*

You want to be really creative

*It didn't have to be like that. It is time,*

*isn't it?*

You are sounding responsible

~

# Turn

*God knows we have cocked things up*

And how do you do that?

*Greed, fear, stupidity*

Greed's a form of fear, coming from

separation

*So you are the answer*

You are the answer

*We have to turn towards you*

Turn towards yourselves – I am

in you

~

# God

*Not the God out there*

The God in here

*Not the God of institutions*

The God of hearts

*Not the God of them*

The God of us

*Not the God of action*

The God of creation

~

# Stroll

*So all we have to do is follow you*
I am following you
*How does that work?*
Exactly the way it has been working
*But it could work better?*
We could walk together
*And how do we do that?*
Fancy a stroll?

~

# Charge

*I thought you were up there*

I am in here

*I thought you were in charge*

Obviously not

*I thought you were letting this happen*

I am

*And why are you doing that?*

Because you are

~

# Creators

*You need to help me here*
I am. You are creators
*You are the creator*
Yes, I am creating through you
*There's a weakness in your plan:*
*we're rubbish!*
No, you are gold-dust
*And you are the alchemist?*
Who else?

~

# Planet

*I still think giving us the keys is a*
*big risk*
To who?
*Well, us, and the planet*
The planet can take care of itself
*What about the other species that*
*we damage*
Species come and go
*So you are betting on us?*
You are betting on you

~

# Process

*Wait for it. We don't have to bet on us*
Who would you rather bet on?
*We can bet on you. That's what you*
*have been saying*
A thought is dawning
*And now is*
This is a continuing process
*Not a one dawn fling*
In your heart

~

# Priests

*The created comes to know the creator*

By working with the creator

*Not from a book?*

Why not work directly?

*Don't we normally go via Priests?*

Human beings like you

*But don't we still need maps?*

Where's your map?

~

# Maps

*I have referred to many maps*
And which of them are you referring
to now?
*None, I'm making my own*
And is that OK?
*It's custom built. Designed for the*
*21st century!*
May it serve you well
*But it doesn't acknowledge*
*other authorities*
It acknowledges me, doesn't it?

~

# Prompts

*I am not sure today's map readers want*
*new maps*
Many people have no map
*What right have I to offer a map?*
It's here for the taking
*I have wanted to have a map for a*
*long time*
But the map is not the territory
*More a series of prompts*
So not that special then?

~

# Nowhere

*You know what the biggest*
*difference is?*
Yes!
*A palpable sense of your presence*
What difference does that make?
*I've stepped inside love*
Where to from here?
*I was going to ask you the*
*same question*
There is nowhere to go

~

# Change

*OK, better resonance, deeper connection*

And what will you do with that?

*That informs life, nothing separate to do*

The connection is life

*But I can still dream*

Are they your dreams?

*Could they be shared?*

They could be deeply connected

~

# Strain

*Take from our hearts the strain*
*and stress!*
When we're connected there's no
strain or stress
*So there's a clue to the absence of you*
The absence of your connection
*Turn up, tune in and connect*
24/7
*Not just when we are in a crisis?*
Why wait for crises?

~

# Holiday

*I feel like I need a break*
Take a holiday
*Good idea*
Make every day a holy day
*And how do we do that?*
Acknowledge your wholeness, get
in touch
*With you*
Through you, with me

~

# Gurus

*The key is to get in touch with the self*
The connected self
*We can't connect through a*
*guru instead?*
You are your self
*But gurus can be helpful*
Way pointers to the self
*And the self is connected to*
Me

~

# Love

*Like everything*

Loving everything is a good plan

*Because everything comes from you*

Because you are love, and love loves

*Except when we are not love*

Then you are caught up in

the drama

*So we must return to love*

There is no other way

~

# Way

*The way is love?*

What else did you think it could be?

*There are as many paths as people*

As many paths to love

*We each have to find our own way*

Actually, you don't

*How is that?*

I will show you

~

# Life

*I'll take it! Really, I'll take it*
I have offered it to you before
*Ouch. Maybe I was not ready*
You are ready
*It feels like I am in a department store*
Life, this way
*OK, I'll buy it*
It was reserved for you

~

# Included

*And everyone else*

Everyone included

*Nobody excluded*

Plenty exclude themselves

*Lost forever?*

Nothing is lost forever

*We can return any time*

It's your order

~

# Child

*Why would I want to do anything else?*

You are trying to prove yourself

*Yes, I see that. I'm an adult*

Try being like a child

*Why would I do that?*

Children appreciate, enjoy, trust

*They also wail*

And what do you do with

your wailings?

~

# Conflict

*We bottle them up inside. We*
*avoid conflict*
You create conflict
*So we should wail?*
Trust and speak honestly
*And be not afraid. We live lives of fear*
You lead lives of separation
*And fighting*
You are still proving yourselves

~

# Inadequacy

*This seems pointless, this*
*proving ourselves*
It's a sign of inadequacy
*But we are not inadequate, right?*
Quite
*It's an adolescent thing*
Not quite sure if you are one thing
or another
*Physical or spirit*
Separate or united

~

# Tuning in

*This, it's all I want to do*
All you want to do
*OK, it's not me, it's us, still I*
*am content*
Then you are not wanting
*Just turning up, just being here*
Tuning in
*As opposed to dropping out*
You are being here

~

# Journey

*Being who I am*

There is no limit to who you are

*No limit to what I can accomplish?*

No limit to who you can know

yourself to be

*Not myself*

In the end the self is everything

*And how does that work?*

Because the self is nothing

~

# Paradox

*Back to paradox again*
The creator and the created
*Separation and unity*
How else could it be?
*In the end there is no end*
Every ending is a beginning
*We are going round in circles*
Would you like to be still?

~

# Still

*Be still and know*

You can find stillness anywhere

*And how do I do that?*

Take a breath

*And in that breath?*

Is everything

*Like a hologram*

Welcome to the hologram

~

# Bidden

*I always have to begin by asking*
*for guidance*
I don't come unbidden
*Can I make a repeat order?*
You are always free to decide
*So it's a going on living thing?*
As you choose
*So let me ask*
I am ready

~

# Version

*Are you God?*

I am your version of God

*Can I have the real thing?*

You know not what you ask

*You reflect my limited understanding?*

I stretch your limited understanding

*I get it*

That may take a while

~

# Waking

*What if everything I've experienced is*
*a dream?*
It is
*And one day I will wake up?*
You are
*I am awake?*
You are stirring
*What will I see?*
You will be the truth

~

# Dreaming

*Thank you for creating this and*
*every moment*
We are creating them together
*What is my part in that?*
You are dreaming them up
*My dreams wouldn't fill a thimble*
*of minutes*
Dream on
*Of what I would wish?*
Of what you would all wish

~

# Live

*A lot of the time I am just*
*dream watching*
You don't remember all of
your dreams
*Yes, it does feel like I have dreamed of*
*this time*
And now you are living it
*So what must I do?*
Nothing. Live the dream. Be more
*I thought I was aiming high*
You were. You are

~

# Lighten

*It's OK to aim to lighten up*
It's more than OK. It's who you are
*I am light?*
Of course. Everything is light
*And lightening up means*
To know the light within
*It try to see that in others*
It's there right in front of you

~

# Words

*I think that something has changed*
You have allowed yourself to
be changed
*I am more in touch with myself*
Your self is more in touch with you
*I am being acted upon?*
There is an interplay
*Life is a play*
On words

~

# Producer

*Words like these?*

This is the word of God

*Woah, hang on*

This, all of existence, is the word

of God

*OK, I am OK with that. And it is*

*for playing*

You are the writer, director and

lead actor

*And you?*

A stage hand. Oh, and the producer

~

# Always

*You had me there for a moment*
I have always had you
*That is just sinking in*
There was never a time when I did
not have you
*That feels like an even bigger statement*
You are eternal too
*What does that mean?*
It means you are not bound by time

~

# Eternal

*Everything exists in time*

You are inside time. And outside it

*How does that work?*

The part that changes lives

inside time

*And the eternal part of me doesn't?*

Where did you think it lived?

*In the eternal present*

Now you are

~

# Adventure

*Sitting here is a bit of an adventure*
The whole thing is, isn't it?
*From its beginning to its end*
And what end do you have
in mind?
*Flow, more flow*
Which isn't really the end
*We're circling*
Reality revolves

~

# Darkness

*We haven't talked about evil*

What do you mean by that?

*Darkness*

Let the light shine

*Who is preventing that?*

You are

*How do we do that?*

See the light, be the light, lighten up

~

# Difference

*You haven't told us how we do darkness*
You feel the difference between light
and dark
*Yes*
Follow the light
*That's that then, pretty straightforward*
More straightforward than
you know
*But I am not sure we always feel*
*the difference*
In the darkness, even a little gloom
feels light
~

# Love-in

*I love you*
And I love you too
*I mean I really get you*
And I really get you too?
*So is this one giant love-in?*
How would you have it be?
*Now you have got me*
Told you so

~

# Sign-up

*I am a little alarmed at how easy this*
*seems to be*
You have been making it hard for a
long time
*So we can really just lighten up*
A time is coming
*Well I sign up, where's the paper?*
Sign up in your heart
*That feels much harder*
Be with me

~

# Goody-goody

*Cut out the guff. Talk and listen*
What could be easier?
*Yet there is more, a little matter*
*of attunement*
Lift up your hearts
*Breath by breath. This feels too*
*goody-goody*
Would you rather have
baddy-baddy?
*I don't think we can suppress what is*
*in us*
You know where I am

~

# Mop

*It still feels like there is too much mess*
*in the world*
Mop it up!
*That's us: mopper uppers?*
Every action is an act of definition
*Of who we are*
Of who you are choosing to be
*I am the choice-maker*
I am the choice-maker

~

# Taker

*I thought it was me who got to make*
*the choices*

I have made every choice possible

*So what is my role?*

Choice-taker

*Junior partner*

Yes

*Then God needs nothing from us*

I am everything

~

# Tango

*I am here again*
And I am here
*Why do I doubt that?*
You don't. You doubt your
connection
*But we are always connected*
I am with you, but you may not be
with me
*It takes two to tango*
It takes you to tango

~

# Suffering

*Can we return to suffering?*

If you wish

*What is the purpose of suffering?*

How do you suffer?

*By resisting. By turning away.*

And the remedy?

*Is to stop resisting, to turn towards you*

Discover yourself and you

discover everything

~

# Choice

*But surely others suffer for*
*other reasons*
How do you know?
*It's obvious in the media*
And you believe that over your
own experience?
*It's plain to see*
You can't see experience, you must
experience it
*We must experience suffering?*
It would seem to be your choice

~

# Presence

*But I am not sure that I am suffering*
*at all*
You know where you are
*So I can choose my own response*
You can be your own creation
*And I feel your presence*
How do you do that?
*I don't do that at all*
Oh yes you do

~

# Let go

*I would call it tuning in*
And how do you do that?
*Get still, get slow, breathe, listen, sense*
*inner space*
And then what happens?
*Stuff surfaces, you may have to let go*
*of all that*
Where does that take you to?
*More space, more freedom, and then I*
*sense peace*
A troubled mind would not have
heard the hush

~

# Hush

*And you are in the hush*
There you will find me
*You are like hush!*
Noise is change, I am the same
*You are the creator of change*
I am the great enabler
*The hush that passeth understanding*
Peace be with you

~

# Carrying

*So we can dip into this peace from time*
*to time*
And why not always?
*I could carry this peace with me every-*
*where I go*
I would be carrying you
*Well, yes, I'll go with that*
And how will you do that?
*Tune in first thing every day and*
*stay there*
Tune-in as you sleep

~

# Tuning in

*Prayers before bed*
Pray throughout the night
*Consciously and unconsciously*
You have been practicing
*I realise it is not for your benefit at all*
Nothing can be for my benefit
*You are already complete*
You are already complete

~

# Everything

*I feel less incomplete*

You lack for nothing

*I know that I have everything I need*

Which is nothing

*For this moment*

And every moment

*Until the end of time*

Amen

~

# Express

*Thank you for being here now*

It's who I am

*Why do I do anything else?*

To express yourself

*And why is that important?*

It's in the nature of being

*If being doesn't do, what is being?*

Being present

~

# Struggles

*OK, I'm back, nothing else but service*
*to you*
Where have you been?
*Getting on, fulfilling commitments,*
*struggling*
Cease all struggles
*Really?*
Come to me all ye who are heavily
burdened
*And I will give you rest*
Come then, come now

~

# Divine

*But there is no place to come*

Just being here now

*And connecting so that it's not me,*

*it's us*

As you remember, it's always us

*In the awareness of that*

Lies the divine

*I have to turn in*

Turn up

~

# Physical

*Why do we have to bother with stuff?*
Your challenges make you complete
*Why should spirit work with*
*the physical?*
It's a great place to become
*And how do we do that?*
Through doing, experience,
reflection
*In other words*
Through who you are choosing to be

~

# Fear

*So many choices feel sub-optimal*
Is that how they felt at the time?
*No, but I have often acted out of fear*
And what, exactly are you
scared of?
*Nothing, right now, nothing*
Fear depends on you
*How does that work?*
Without you, fear does not exist

~

# Love Fear

*I am the source of my fears?*

Without your acquiescence, they

cannot be

*So I can reject them all?*

You can see them for what they are

*And what is that?*

Aspects of yourself

*And how should I respond to them*

Love your fears

~

# Gone

*That feels counter-intuitive*

You cannot resist fears

*Why not?*

All resistance is fearful

*So we should go with everything?*

Flow with everything

*And how does that work?*

Everything that flows is gone

~

# Lighter

*I do not need to know the way*

You know the way, you are upon
the way

*I am in the way*

You are being who you choose to be

*A way maker*

It is already made

*A way lighter*

Why would you hide your light?

~

# Converse

*I wish everyone could have this kind*
*of conversation*
Everyone converses in their
own way
*Yes, but not everyone has this kind of*
*conversation*
Everyone converses in their
own way
*You always listen*
And there is always a response
*How do you respond?*
What do you think the world is?

~

# Waiting

*A place to hang out while we wait for*
*something better*
This is it, the time is now
*We shouldn't wait for something better?*
Engage with the process
*Stop procrastinating?*
Know it, feel it, be it
*Know, feel, be what?*
Oh ye of little faith

~

# Hard

*So we should stop waiting and ...*

Dream your dreams, live your

dreams

*Create with you*

I have given you the tools

*But it feels hard*

Hard is just feedback

*Which tells us?*

That there is a better way to be

~

# Feelings

*So when it feels difficult, we should just turn around?*
Really look at the difficult feeling and you see
*See what?*
That it is within you
*But the difficulty is out there*
The feeling is within
*So we work on our feelings*
You change the world through your feelings

~

# Mist

*Don't we also change things through*
*our focus?*
And your focus depends on
your feelings
*A lot of the time we don't really*
*feel anything*
A lot of the time you aren't
going anywhere
*Our feelings are our compass!*
We can go with that
*But our left-over feelings are like a mist*
Connect with the present

~

# Ways

*We should not be doing this, you know*
Because
*We should be communicating*
*through religions*
But I am in you and you are in me
*But it would seem to some wildly*
*inappropriate*
They aren't here
*They are going their way*
It's the same way

~

# Hanging

*I have to wait upon you*
You have to do no such thing
*I choose to wait upon you*
You choose to notice divine
promptings
*That are here all the time*
You are getting the hang of it
*I am hanging in here*
You have no place else to go

~

# Exhaustion

*This is where I have to be?*

Nowhere else makes sense to you

any more

*So I turn up out of desperation?*

Does it feel like that?

*No, but there is a sense of having*

*exhausted options*

Or exhausted yourself

*OK, you win*

There is only one winner here

~

# One

*I like the ambiguity*

There is ambiguity in separation

*Because there is none*

Except as it is experienced

*The one contains the parts*

All is one

*Everything is a part*

Of the one

~

# Soup

*I want to feel the connection with everything*
Then lose yourself
*Why is that necessary?*
Because the self gets in the way
*Our parochial concerns*
Your sense of separateness
*I am just part of the soup*
You are the soup

~

# Being

*So I have to be not me*

You have to be we

*And then I am connected*

And what they connect

*I have transcended the self*

You are not yourself

*I know who I am!?*

You know who we are

~

# Sensing[1]

*I sense that I am*

And who are you?

*The one sensing*

The only one sensing?

*The only one sensing what I*

*am sensing*

I am sensing too

*What are you sensing?*

I am sensing everything

~

# Experience

*You are here with me sensing what I
am sensing*
Did you think I had gone away?
*And you are sensing everything!*
Why did you think I created this
whole show?
*To see how we would get on?*
To experience the whole thing
*And how does that work?*
I experience creation

~

# In

*If we are both here, what is distinctive*
*about me?*
Everything: there is only one you
*And where do I stop and you start?*
You don't stop. And I don't start
*I am in you and you are in me?*
Where did you think you were?
*I see that I cannot be anywhere else*
And where do you think I am?

~

# Not you

*You are everywhere!*

Which means I am in you

*I am not where you are, not everywhere.*

You are not really you

*I beg your pardon*

You are just having the experience

of being you

*I am the experiencer*

Yes, we are

~

# Embarked

*Who is the me is having the experience
of being me?*
You are getting close to
understanding the riddle
*Help me with this*
You will have to understand
yourself
*A life's work!*
You have embarked upon it
*Did I have a choice?*
We'll return to that

~

# Joined

*OK, tell me who I am*
You aren't really you at all
*There's no me*
There is no separateness
*Only a sense of separateness*
There's only we
*We are joined*
One being one

~

# Apartness

*Can we have it both ways?*

You can have it the way you want it

*Be separate and be together*

Which is exactly what you

are experiencing

*But the reality is?*

You experience a part of the reality

*And what is that?*

Apartness

~

# Envelope

*But I am starting to experience*
*joinedupness*
And how does that feel?
*There's a touchable out-there-ness: like*
*a cloud*
Enveloping all
*And an in-here-ness. Gloriously*
*unsettling*
Vibrant life, burgeoning forwards
*And yet flowing beautifully*
A revelry

~

# Serve

*My wish is to serve you: they will*
*be done*
And how will you do that?
*By listening to you*
And why do you wish to serve me?
*You are the life force. When I serve you,*
*I serve life*
When you serve life, you serve me
*And life, what is that?*
An expression of me

~

# Jesus

*Let's talk about Jesus*

Why not talk to Jesus?

*He's here now?*

Where did you think he would be?

*So I can talk with him?*

Millions do

*Really?*

As well as they may

~

# Together

*How could they talk better with Jesus*
Stop thinking of yourself as separate
*As separate from you?*
As separate from one another
*And Jesus and the Saints?*
Get over this separation thing
*Stop putting ourselves down?*
Why would you do that?

~

# Embrace

*Because we know we are being less*
*than ourselves*
You are so much more than
yourselves
*Back to Jesus?*
I am in the father and the father is
in me
*There is an understanding of connection*
It is the father in me that does
the works
*That it would be so*
Embrace the truth and it will
embrace you

~

# Realize

*Does that mean giving up ourselves?*

It means realizing that you

weren't you

*The death of the self*

The end of separateness

*We know that realization changes every-*

*thing?*

Realization is everything

*It's what we are here to do?*

You aren't here to do

~

# Self-manifesting

*There are any number of things to do*
Limitless opportunities to express
who you are
*That's it. Action is a manifestation*
*of being*
You thought they weren't
connected?
*I am content, being, except when I*
*am not*
You are pulled this way and that
*I lose sight of the path*
It is before you

~

# Splash

*And what have I to do to see it?*

Connect, only connect

*I know when things are clear and when*

*they are not*

And how do you handle that?

*When things aren't clear, I usually*

*thrash about a bit*

What effect does that have?

*A lot of splashing*

You know that you float

~

# Closer

*Direct my life*

You don't mean that

*I am getting closer*

There is a learning experience

*You mean I can learn from my mistakes*

You are evolving

*I feel that I am gradually recognizing*

*who I am*

Bingo

~

# Unlimited

*But it still feels to me that life is*
*a struggle*
Yes, you are struggling
*It feels that they have more power*
*than me*
You have unlimited power
*But that is also rather scary*
And what, precisely, are you
scared of?
*That I am not using my talents to*
*achieve my purpose*
One step at a time

~

# Hope

*There is hope. I feel encouraged*
O ye of little faith
*Again, alright, I have some faith*
And what does that look like?
*Troubles aren't real. Everything will*
*turn out well*
And …
*You are with me always*
Even unto the ends of time

~

# Rut

*And there is no limit to my stupidity*
And no limit to who you can be
*Except for all the limits I place*
*upon myself*
And why would you do that?
*Remaining in a familiar rut*
You are allowed to pause
*It's time to move on*
Why would you want to do that?

~

# Shame

*Shame, shame makes me want to*
*move on*
Then shame can be useful
*As a species, we aren't doing that well*
Look at what you have conquered
and controlled
*And that is to our credit?*
It's a phase you have been
going through
And the next phase?
Let go of it all

~

# Share

*How can we get stuff done when we don't control it?*

You can share it. Your life can be an example

*How can we share it if we don't have it?*

You already have everything

*Share with everyone? We would soon run out*

Share your talents

*Won't we run out of income?*

Do you think your talents are yours?

~

# Talents

*Our talents aren't ours?*

You have borrowed them

*We have to return them?*

You have to return everything

*But we are responsible for their use*

Why do you think you have them?

*Better get on with it?*

You have time

~

# Stream

I am a bit concerned the we

are meandering

Like a stream

That flows into the sea

And that is not the end of the story

The sea forms clouds from where

droplets fall

Ingenious, don't you think?

And I am in a stream

You are a droplet, a stream, a cloud

~

# Deliver

*And let's focus on you*

How do you experience me?

*I could say in every breath*

Why not?

*And I experience your responsiveness*

And how do you do that?

*I ask and you deliver*

So I am a delivery man?

~

# Someone

*You have set the whole thing up.*

*Someone had to*

The creator

*And though you are beyond our*

*experience ...*

I am your experience

*OK, we can experience you*

You cannot not experience me

*We can experience the flow that*

*you offer*

As you like

~

# Drama

*I still have a penchant for drama*
Your dramas serve a purpose
*And what is that?*
To move beyond the drama
*Why not move beyond the*
*drama anyway?*
Why not, indeed
*I enjoy them. Need them. Get*
*swallowed up in them.*
What would you gain if you
lost them?

~

# Everything

*I would gain you, I do gain you*
*The self, the whole self, and nothing*
*but the self*
Which you are anyway going to lose
*When I am ready*
All resistance is fearful
*So we should go with everything?*
Flow with everything
*And how does that work?*
Everything that flows is gone

~

# Found

*Thank you for every moment*
Present
*It's you, almighty you, I feel it.*
And it is like
*Floating on a cloud, even while in*
*this body*
And your cup brimmeth over
*A happy surrender*
Found!

~

# Shine

*I hear you say*
So what is your wish?
*It makes me feel that I am in the*
*driving seat?*
Every moment is sent to you
*Thank you for each one*
And how would you like to do that?
*By being an enlightener*
Let your light shine

~

# Blowing

*I appreciate that I am nothing*
You are a part of everything
*I am a wayward spirit blowing in*
*the wind*
You are a part of me
*Unreliable, inconsistent, but willing to*
*be inspired*
And be inspirational
*Yes!*
It's time

~

# Butterfly

*A quantum leap in my life*
And what will be different?
*Continually open to your promptings*
Like a butterfly[2]
*Emerging from the shell and flying*
Faithfully
*On auto-pilot*
Feeling your way

~

# Changed

*Thank you for becoming more and*
*more real*
Know who you are
*I am getting more of it*
Why have you been holding back?
*A lack of faith in myself*
And what has changed?
*The experience of something greater*
That will do

~

# Continuity Note

That's it. It's over, still curious?
Some of you who read *Why You Are
Here – Briefly* asked for a little more
explanation. After some years of
wanting to represent spiritual truths
in a simpler form, these dialogues
started drifting into my awareness:
as I walked through a park one
would pop in. This time they are all
8-lines long "octologues". The next
title in the series is *Finding
Your Truth.*
www.knockknockwhosgod.org

# B O O K S

O is a symbol of the world, of oneness and unity. In different cultures it also means the "eye," symbolizing knowledge and insight. We aim to publish books that are accessible, constructive and that challenge accepted opinion, both that of academia and the "moral majority."

Our books are available in all good English language bookstores worldwide. If you don't see the book on the shelves ask the bookstore to order it for you, quoting the ISBN number and title. Alternatively you can order online (all major online retail sites carry our titles) or contact the distributor in the relevant country, listed on the copyright page.

See our website www.o-books.net for a full list of over 500 titles, growing by 100 a year.

And tune in to myspiritradio.com for our book review radio show, hosted by June-Elleni Laine, where you can listen to the authors discussing their books.